"Where can we Christians find reliable answers to our common questions about life together at church—without having to plow through long, expensive books? The Church Questions booklets meet our need with answers that are biblical, thoughtful, and practical. For pastors, this series will prove a trustworthy resource for guiding church members toward deeper wisdom and stronger unity."

Ray Ortlund, President, Renewal Ministries

What Do Deacons Do?

Church Questions

What Do Deacons Do?

Juan Sanchez

CROSSWAY®

WHEATON, ILLINOIS

Trade paperback ISBN: 978-1-4335-7900-4
ePub ISBN: 978-1-4335-7903-5
PDF ISBN: 978-1-4335-7901-1
Mobipocket ISBN: 978-1-4335-7902-8

Library of Congress Cataloging-in-Publication Data

Names: Sánchez, Juan, 1954- author.
Title: What do deacons do? / Juan Sanchez.
Description: Wheaton, Illinois : Crossway, 2022. | Series: Church questions |Includes bibliographical references and index.
Identifiers: LCCN 2021027448 (print) | LCCN 2021027449 (ebook) | ISBN 9781433579004 (trade paperback) | ISBN 9781433579011 (pdf) | ISBN 9781433579028 (mobipocket) | ISBN 9781433579035 (epub)
Subjects: LCSH: Deacons.
Classification: LCC BV680 .S24 2022 (print) | LCC BV680 (ebook) | DDC 253—dc23
LC record available at https://lccn.loc.gov/2021027448
LC ebook record available at https://lccn.loc.gov/2021027449

Crossway is a publishing ministry of Good News Publishers.

BP		31	30	29	28	27	26	25	24	23	22
15	14	13	12	11	10	9	8	7	6	5	4	3	2	1

Therefore, brothers, pick out from among you seven men of good repute, full of the Spirit and of wisdom, whom we will appoint to this duty.

Acts 6:3

As a pastor, I've received some odd requests from church members, but none have been quite as odd as the request James and John made of Jesus in Mark 10: "Teacher, we want you to do for us whatever we ask of you" (Mark 10:35). Now that's bold! I'm not sure what I'd do if a church member asked me that. I'd probably tell them to go away.

But Jesus is kinder than I am. He plays along and asks what they want him to do. Their request gets even more provocative: "Grant us to sit, one at your right hand and one at your left, in your glory" (Mark 10:37).

As you might imagine, the other apostles didn't respond well to James and John's hubris. In fact, they were "indignant" with them (Mark 10:41). Jumping into the fray—and probably stopping a few folks from coming to blows—Jesus quells the indignation of his apostles and then teaches them all a lesson about true greatness.

> And Jesus called them to him and said to them, "You know that those who are considered rulers of the Gentiles lord it over them, and their great ones exercise authority over them. But it shall not be so among you. But whoever would be great among you must be your servant, and whoever would be first among you must be slave of all." (Mark 10:42–44)

The *greatest* in the kingdom are *servants*. The world thinks greatness corresponds to power, but in God's eyes greatness corresponds to service—particularly serving the people of God.

The Bible regularly emphasizes the centrality of "service" in the Christian life. For instance,

Paul commanded the early Christians to use their freedoms to "serve one another" (Gal. 5:13). Likewise, Peter commanded his readers: "As each has received a gift, use it to serve one another, as good stewards of God's varied grace" (1 Pet. 4:10).

And yet, we all know from experience that service is hard, sometimes grueling work. Even more, it's hard to know how to serve others in a way that *actually* helps.

But did you know that the Lord does more than simply tell his people to serve each other? He cares so deeply about this that he actually gives his church living examples of how to serve. These super-servants *lead* others to serve others effectively and fruitfully.

These people are called deacons.

The word "deacon" means different things to different people depending on their church tradition and personal experiences. Growing up in the Roman Catholic Church, I thought deacons were seminarians training for the priesthood. At the end of my senior year in high school, I came to faith in Christ through the witness of some

Southern Baptist classmates. In that context, deacons were the spiritual and administrative leaders of the church; they helped the pastor make important decisions. During college, I served in several churches in part-time student ministry positions. These years were marked by "deacon board meetings," which reinforced my perception that deacons were the church's spiritual and administrative leaders.

But as I continued in ministry and continued to read the Bible, I discovered that none of my experiences seemed to match what the Bible says about deacons. I realized that Scripture's portrayal of deacons—though sparse—was far more glorious and beautiful than anything I'd witnessed. I began to see the wisdom in how Jesus had structured his church and the vital role that deacons play in the life of the church and in the great commission.

Like me, you've probably had questions about deacons—that's why you picked up this little book. In the next few pages, I hope to answer some of those questions by walking with you through the relevant biblical texts. My aim is simple: I want you to embrace what the Bible teaches about this topic—after all, God's opinion is the only one that really matters. I only wish to serve as a guide.

But more than that, I want these truths to shape the way you live out your devotion to Christ. If you're not a deacon, I hope this book teaches you to appreciate the way that Jesus has ordered the church. I hope you'll see how you can promote your church's gospel witness by supporting the work of your deacons. Even more, I hope that some of you will be inspired by Scripture's glorious depiction of deacon ministry and aspire to become deacons yourselves.

If you're already a deacon in your church, I hope this little book reminds you of your high calling and encourages you to continue serving with excellence and faithfulness. Perhaps it will also offer a few course corrections along the way.

Almost every church has deacons. So my goal in this book is to help every church member see how deacons serve the church, why their ministry is indispensable, and how the whole church can value and support their work.

What Is a Deacon?

My first pastorate began with a conflict about deacons. The church recognized the deacons as spiritual leaders. They were, after all, older and wiser men who were successful in both life and business. But I had become convinced from Scripture that deacons weren't meant to serve as spiritual leaders in the church. Servant-leadership belongs to the elders. The deacons engage in a different type of service. They serve the administrative and physical needs of the congregation; modeling the practical, tangible ways that all church members can serve one another.[1]

But I knew enough not to make significant changes before the church was ready.

I took the deacons on a retreat where we studied the pastoral epistles together (1 and 2 Timothy and Titus). We worked through Paul's letters and noted the varied responsibilities he gave to elders and deacons. I simply wanted us to learn together from Scripture what we were called to do—I, as the pastor; they, as the deacons. It sounded like a great idea. Sadly . . . it didn't go over so well—at least with the chairman of the deacons. He calmly entered my study the following Monday and offered his resignation. Not a great start for a new pastor!

How did I offend this brother to the point of resignation? Well, I had pointed out that the Bible established pastors (also called "elders" in Scripture) to serve the church by teaching and leading. Deacons, meanwhile, were called to a different type of service: meeting the tangible needs of the congregation. He was convinced that I was trying to marginalize the deacons and set myself up as the church's sole authority.

This brother was half-right and half-wrong. He was right that church leadership *is* shared leadership. But he was wrong because this leadership isn't shared between two balancing "houses"—an elder board and a deacon board. It's shared between elders equally. That's why every church should have multiple elders or pastors (Titus 1:5). In short, he had confused the office of deacon with the office of pastor.

As we'll see, confusing those two different offices can have disastrous effects on the church. Scripture shows us that deacons have one particular calling in life and pastors have another—neither is better than the other and each gloriously reflects something of the character of Christ.

So let's get to it. What is a deacon? Knowing what a deacon *is* will help us better understand what a deacon *does*.

In the most general sense, a *deacon* is one who serves. In fact, our English word "deacon" comes from the Greek word for "service" (*diakonos*). So from one perspective, all Christians are *deacons* (Matt. 20:26; 23:11). The Bible even refers to different types of ministry as *deacon* work, or "deaconing"—if we can make up a word. For example, pastors are called to "equip the saints for the work of ministry [*diakonias*]" (Eph. 4:12). Some Christians are gifted in service (*diakonian*), and they are encouraged to serve (*diakonia*) (Rom. 12:7).

Our focus in this book, however, is on the use of the term *deacon* in a more specific sense— "Deacon" with a capital D, deacon as an office in the church. The noun *deacon* is only used in this sense a couple times in Scripture. When addressing the Philippian church, Paul greets "all the saints . . . with the overseers and *deacons*" (Phil. 1:1). Additionally, writing to Timothy, Paul explains the qualifications for *deacons* in 1 Timothy 3:8–12. He concludes those qualifications by reminding Timothy and his church: "Those who serve well as deacons gain a good standing for themselves and also great confidence in the faith that is in Christ Jesus (1 Tim. 3:13).

To summarize, then, all Christians are servants, but some Christians serve in a specific office of "deacon." In this sense, a *deacon* is an official servant recognized by the church. But this raises a question: If all Christians are deacons, then why does a church need to recognize "official" deacons?

Why Churches Need Deacons

Before we talk about why a church needs deacons, let's do a little crash course on what a church is and what it's supposed to do.

When Jesus asked Peter and the apostles, "Who do you say that I am?" Peter answered, "You are the Christ, the Son of the living God" (Matt. 16:15–16). Peter didn't come up with this answer on his own. Our heavenly Father revealed to him and the other apostles that Jesus was the promised King who would save his people from their sins (v. 17). On the foundation of this gospel confessor confessing this gospel message, Jesus builds his church (v. 18).

The Great Commission makes this point plainly:

> Go therefore and make disciples of all nations, baptizing them in the name of the Father and of the Son and of the Holy Spirit, teaching them to observe all that I have commanded you. And behold, I am with you always, to the end of the age." (Matt. 28:19–20)

Because Jesus is King, we are to go into the world under his authority and with his presence to preach his gospel. All who repent and believe the good news about Jesus are to be baptized and gathered into local churches. In those churches, Christians teach one another how to follow Jesus and obey all he has commanded.

Jesus has structured his church to make sure it stays true to that mission. According to Ephesians 4:11, the ascended Christ has given to the church "apostles and prophets" (the foundation of the church), "evangelists" (those who preach the gospel where Christ is not named), and "shepherds and teachers" (those responsible to teach the gospel in the church). The purpose of shepherds and teachers is "to equip the saints for the work of ministry [*diakonia*], for building up the body of Christ" (Eph. 4:12). In other words, pastors teach church members how to be faithful Christians, and in turn those church members encourage one another and share the gospel with the lost. So the pastors live according to and teach all that Jesus commanded, the church members obey all that Jesus commanded, and in this way unbelievers are brought to faith and the church is built up to look more like Jesus. The structure of the church supports the mission of the church.

Now to the question: How do deacons fit into that picture?

Well, it turns out that maintaining the priority of preaching the gospel isn't easy. Pastors are often bombarded with problems that threaten to consume their time and turn their attention away from gospel preaching. So that's where deacons come in. They play a vital role in making sure local churches keep gospel-preaching at the heart of their mission.

We see this clearly in Acts 6.

Let's set the context. After Peter preached the gospel in Jerusalem, three thousand people believed and were added to the church (Acts 2:41). Jesus continued to build his church daily through the preaching of this word (Acts 2:47). By the time we get to Acts 6, there are well over five thousand Christians in the Jerusalem church.

As you might expect, the church experienced some growing pains, and a conflict emerged. The Greek-speaking widows were being neglected in the daily distribution of food (Acts 6:1). Until this point, the apostles had handled much of the administrative responsibilities themselves (Acts 5). But it became clear that if they took on this new problem, they would have to neglect the ministry of the word (Acts 6:2). To protect the priority of teaching and preaching, they offered a practical solution: "Pick out from among you seven men of good repute, full of the Spirit and of wisdom, whom we will appoint to this duty" (Acts 6:3).

This solution pleased the whole congregation (Acts 6:5) and allowed the apostles to prioritize preaching and prayer (Acts 6:4). Luke tells us what happened as a result: "The word of God continued to increase, and the number of the disciples multiplied greatly in Jerusalem, and a great many of the priests became obedient to the faith" (Acts 6:7).

While these seven men aren't called deacons, they certainly served in a *diaconal* role. They were model servants set aside by the entire congregation to fulfill a particular task—that's exactly what deacons do today.

Acts 6 provides a beautifully balanced picture for the different types of service that animate a healthy church. The apostles *served* through the ministry of the word and prayer. The deacons *served* the church by meeting physical and administrative needs. Acts 6 is also a compelling picture for why the church needs deacons. A problem arose in the church that threatened both the priority of the ministry of the word and the church's unity. How did the church respond to this crisis? By appointing deacons.

These deacons *protected* and *prioritized* the church's preaching and teaching ministry. When the practical needs of the church threatened to overwhelm the apostles' time, the deacons stepped in to care for those needs. When divisions started creeping into the church, the deacons stepped in to create peace between emerging factions.

So let's put together what we have so far. A *deacon* is an official servant recognized by the church to help the pastors *protect* and *prioritize* the church's mission by meeting tangible needs. They also help *preserve* and *promote* the church's unity.

It's a glorious picture, isn't it? It's one that I've had the privilege of witnessing firsthand in my own life and ministry. When we instituted deacons at High Pointe Baptist Church where I serve as lead pastor, we tasked Carlos, one of our most faithful, longest-serving members, to coordinate our care of widows and shut-ins. He was a trusted man in the congregation. He made people smile and brought a lot of joy into others' lives.

With the help of his wife Josie, Carlos immediately set out to recruit other couples to form a ministry team. Carlos and his team were so effective that it became common for an elder to make a hospital visit only to learn that Carlos and Josie had already been there. It became common for the elders to hear of a shut-in member's needs, only to discover someone from Carlos's team had already met them.

By making sure our widows and shut-ins were cared for, Carlos and his team freed up the elders to prioritize the ministry of the word and prayer. They performed their duties with joy and took their role seriously, knowing they were doing God's work and God would reward them.

But Carlos and his team weren't just freeing up the elders, they were also preserving and promoting the unity of the church. When one of our elders made a pastoral visit to a shut-in, she beamed as she described how Carlos and his team had visited her regularly and cared for her well. During that same visit, she complained that "the pastor" had not come by to visit with her like Carlos had. This pastor reminded her of the size of our church and the need to protect the priority of the word. He gently reminded her that "the pastor" could not be all things to all members—we established deacons to make sure she was cared for.

With this little bit of discipling, she understood that the elders were, in fact, caring for her by establishing deacons like Carlos who fulfilled their diaconal ministry with excellence. By continuing to visit her and other shut-ins and widows, our members have learned that the ministry of the deacons is an extension of the ministry of the elders to care for the flock of God.

How Do Deacons Carry Out Their Job?

When I came to High Pointe Baptist Church in 2005, the elders met from 7:00 pm until past midnight . . . *every* Monday! Why? Because there were many problems facing the church. As a result, though our membership was fifteen hundred, attendance had dwindled down to about three hundred on Sundays. We had $4.5 million in debt we couldn't service. So every Monday, the chairman of the elders came into the church office to decide which bills would be paid. Added to this, we had the burden of caring for our remaining members while also prioritizing the preaching of the word. The elders were essentially doing everything from pastoral care to finances to making sure the building was maintained. It was too much for a handful of men to keep up with.

In other words, we needed deacons!

We've seen that the early church established deacons to preserve the unity of the church and to guard the priority of the elders' teaching and preaching ministry. But *how exactly* do they do this?

1. Deacons Serve the Church

As already mentioned, service is at the heart of being a deacon; it's the overarching job description. Their service must spring from a Spirit-filled heart that loves Christ and his people.

2. Deacons Take Initiative

Deacons don't just wait around until something bad happens. They sniff out potential problems and initiate solutions. They see needs and look for ways to meet them.

3. Deacons Organize Others

Some problems or issues may be solved relatively quickly. If you see trash in the parking lot when you leave the Sunday service, pick it up and throw it in a receptacle. Some matters, however, require more time, planning, and people. With God-given wisdom, deacons can recruit other servants to join them in their efforts.

Too often, deacons tackle problems alone. Think of a church that has a deacon of building and grounds. Every time a toilet is broken or the trees need trimming or the auditorium needs painting, he's the one to do all the work. Not only is this inefficient, he ends up cheating others out of opportunities to serve. Because deacons have a good reputation in the church, they can recruit a team of servants and organize them to solve problems.

4. Deacons Preserve and Promote Church Unity

Church unity is rooted in God's supernatural saving work. Jesus has brought us into the same family through his blood (Eph. 2:11–22). Unity is a gift we receive through the ministry of the Holy Spirit (Eph. 4:1–3). And it's a testimony we give as we reflect the image of the triune God (Eph. 4:4–6). We must eagerly maintain this unity because it displays the wisdom of God's plan to unite a fractured humanity in Christ (Eph. 3:8–10).

Deacons play a vital role in preserving and promoting that unity by spotting threats and finding solutions that preserve peace. Deacons also promote the church's unity by organizing brothers and sisters to serve one another in the church.

5. Deacons Assist the Elders

While deacons serve the church, as we saw in Acts 6, they also have a specific part in protecting and prioritizing the mission of the church. They do so by assisting the elders so that the elders can prioritize the ministry of the word and prayer.[2]

You may have noticed that I am assuming a model of church leadership where there is a plurality of elders. While this is not a booklet on elders, to better understand the role of deacons and how they serve the church by assisting the elders, I need to take a moment to explain the relationship between these two biblical offices.[3]

The New Testament indicates that local churches should be overseen by a group of men who "shepherd" the congregation. Throughout Scripture these men are referred to as "pastors" or "elders"—two words that refer to the same office of leadership (Acts 15:2; 20:17; 21:18; 1 Tim. 4:14; 5:17; Titus 1:5; James 5:14; 1 Pet. 5:1). Scripture charges pastors, or elders, with the teaching ministry of the church.[4] The pastoral office isn't just some "best business practice" the apostle Paul dreamt up. No, the ascended Christ has structured his church this way and gives elders as gifts to his church (Eph. 4:11). By this structure, Jesus means to protect and prioritize the mission of the church.

When deacons protect the elders' time and ministry and prioritize the church's mission, the word continues to grow and spread (Acts 6:7). Think about that! If we care about the spread of the gospel, then we should care about deacons doing what the Bible instructs them to do. When deacons serve, the gospel spreads.

When a church confuses the offices of elders and deacons, problems emerge. For example, in a church where the deacons are the church's spiritual leaders, who's responsible for the teaching ministry? Deacons or "the pastor"? If the deacons are responsible, then who's identifying and caring for the needs of the congregation? On the other hand, consider what happens when a church has only elders but no deacons. Who's organizing others to care for the church's physical needs and thereby getting distracted from prayer and the ministry of the word?

Based on my ministry experience for the last two decades, this is a revolutionary way of thinking about deacons for many churches. Rather than a "deacon board" that makes spiritual and administrative decisions alongside the pastor, this approach to deacons as recognized servants is more task-specific. These tasks may be permanent. For example, a "deacon of ordinances" may oversee a team that prepares for the Lord's Supper and baptisms on Sundays. But they also may be temporary or short-term. For example, a deacon may coordinate a specific construction project or seasonal event.

It's important to note, though, that a church shouldn't have deacons just to have deacons. Remember, Jesus has structured his church so that the structure will serve the mission. It's possible that in a new church plant, the elders will do most of the work themselves—initiating, organizing, meeting needs, just like the apostles did early in their ministry (Acts 5). But as soon as those elders realize that their priority of the word is slipping, they need to consider raising up and identifying faithful members to serve as deacons.

But who *exactly* should they look for? Thankfully, Scripture answers this question for us.

Who Can Be a Deacon?

In Acts 6, the apostles didn't just grab the first church members to volunteer. They chose "seven men of good repute, full of the Spirit and of wisdom" (Acts 6:3). Though all Christians are deacons in a general sense, those identified by the church must be qualified. That was true in Acts 6, and it becomes even clearer in 1 Timothy and Titus.

Writing to Timothy, Paul explains to his young pastor-friend what kind of person can serve as a deacon. Like elders or pastors, deacons should be Christians with blameless character who hold to biblical convictions and lovingly care for the church (1 Tim. 3:8–13). Anyone can set up chairs in an auditorium. Most members may serve in the nursery. We can all pitch in during a workday to do landscaping. But those entrusted to serve in an official capacity must be seen *by the church* as people of godly character, biblical conviction, and loving care.[5]

For that reason, Scripture offers qualifications for deacons (1 Tim 3:8–12). These qualifications focus on character, not competence. Let's take a look.

Deacons Are Trustworthy

> Deacons likewise must be dignified, not double-tongued, not addicted to much wine, not greedy for dishonest gain. (1 Tim. 3:8)

If deacons solve the problems that potentially threaten the mission and unity of the church, they must be trusted by the congregation. Godly people gain a good name or reputation over time. But if someone is "double-tongued"—that is, if someone talks out of both sides of his mouth—he can't be trusted with members' private concerns. If someone is "addicted to much wine," he can't be trusted to serve the church wisely and reliably. If someone is "greedy for dishonest gain," he can't be trusted with any financial matters.

In short, we must be able to trust those who help us.

Deacons Maintain Biblical Convictions

> They must hold the mystery of the faith with a clear conscience. (1 Tim. 3:9)

Whenever members need the deacons' help, they will also need biblical counsel. Whether the need is material, financial, or physical, it will almost always accompany some need of biblical truth. When Christians struggle, they tend to question God's sovereignty, God's goodness, or both.

That's why deacons must not only be equipped to offer physical care, they also need to be able to minister the truth of God's word. I don't mean that they need to be able to preach a 30-minute sermon. But they need to be able to pray biblically informed prayers. They need to be able to make biblically informed decisions. To do that, they "must hold the mystery of the faith" (that is, the gospel that has been revealed in Christ's coming) with a clear conscience (that is, without hypocrisy).

Deacons Must Have a Proven, Blameless Character That Has Been Tested over Time

> And let them also be tested first; then let them serve as deacons if they prove themselves blameless. (1 Tim. 3:10)

It's hard to know if someone is credible the first time you meet them. When it comes to elders, Paul advises us to slow down before recognizing them. Why? Because some people can hide their sins for a season. But eventually, it usually rises to the surface. On the other hand, some people's good works aren't noticeable initially. But eventually, they emerge into view (1 Tim. 5:22, 24–25).

That's good counsel, and it applies to deacons as well. How do you know if someone has godly character? How can you tell if someone holds to biblical convictions or if they care for hurting church members? You observe it over time.

Deacons Practice Loving Care

> Let deacons each be the husband of one wife, managing their children and their own households well. (1 Tim. 3:12)

Deacons must care for the congregation. How can we determine if someone knows how to care well for others and can serve as a deacon? We look at how they treat their families. How deacons care for their families shows the church how they will care for others. Additionally, caring for a family also requires administration and organization (managing)—essential skills for deacons.

Once again, I've seen firsthand how godly, qualified deacons help the church's ministry. Sadly, I've also seen how unqualified deacons can harm it. My own church is the result of a church merger. When we reestablished deacons as one church, we were told of men who had previously served in that capacity. Foolishly, we assumed that because "Jack" had previously worked as a deacon, he was qualified to serve again. But his hidden sins eventually emerged. At Jack's previous church, deacons didn't have specific tasks. We assumed that our task-specific approach to deacons would enable Jack to serve his new church well.

Boy, were we wrong! Jack still had an old mindset of what a deacon should do. He assumed he had some sort of general authority in the church. Rather than join us when we gathered for worship on Sunday mornings, he roamed the halls greeting folks and conversing with volunteers. Not only did Jack not value gathering with God's people, other significant sin patterns also began to emerge in his life. Sadly, we had to remove Jack from his office and insist that he stop forsaking the assembly of God's people.

One of our elders still meets with Jack regularly, but at this point we don't know how his story will end. We learned the hard way that deacons must have godly character proven over time. Slow processes protect the church. They allow sin to be exposed, and they allow faithfulness to be revealed (1 Tim. 5:22–25).

A Common Question: Can Women Be Deacons?

Before continuing, I want to take a moment to address a common question: Can women be deacons? You may have noticed in our discussion about deacon qualifications that I skipped over 1 Timothy 3:11. Faithful, godly Christians differ on whether this verse prohibits or allows women deacons.[6]

Personally, I was convinced for a long time that only men could serve as deacons. But, as I've continued to study Scripture, I've changed my view. I now believe women can serve in this capacity as well.

But let me offer a few words of pastoral wisdom and care. If your church has women deacons, consider whether they're acting according to the biblical model of a deacon: acting as servants, not church leaders.[7]

If a church is going to have women deacons, then it must also have a clear understanding of biblical manhood and womanhood. Men and women are both equally made in God's image, yet God has designed them to have different roles in the home (Genesis 1–2). The godly man leads with loving authority, and the godly wife follows voluntarily with encouraging submission (Eph. 5:22–33). This pattern established in the garden before the fall should be maintained in the church (1 Tim. 2:11–15).

For this reason, Scripture teaches that only qualified men should be pastors because they have been tasked by Jesus, the chief shepherd, with the authority to teach and lead the church.[8] So, in places where deacons function as the spiritual leaders of the church, women shouldn't serve as deacons.

A High and Holy Calling: How Diaconal Service Shows Us the Character of Christ

It's a bit of a shocking claim, but deacons actually show us something of the character of

Christ himself. I began this book with the story in Mark 10 of Jesus teaching the disciples "whoever would be great among you must be your servant" (v. 43).

But I didn't quote *all* of Jesus's words. Notice what he says next:

> But whoever would be great among you must be your servant [*diakonos*], and whoever would be first among you must be slave of all. *For even the Son of Man came not to be* served [*diakonethenai*] *but to serve* [*diakonesai*], *and to give his life as a ransom for many."* (Mark 10:43–45)

The Lord Jesus Christ is the model for all deacons. This shouldn't surprise us. After all, the prophet Isaiah regularly refers to the coming Messiah as the "*servant*" of the Lord (Isa. 42:1; 52:13–53:12). As my friend Matt Smethurst says, "Jesus is both King of kings and Deacon of deacons."[9]

If you're not a deacon, remember that when you witness deacons serving in your church, you are seeing a reflection of Christ's humble, servant-hearted character. That thought should not only stir more affection in your heart for Christ, it should also move you to spend more time encouraging the deacons in your church and imitating their ways of life. Follow them as they follow Christ. Mimic their servant-hearted example and follow their leadership as you seek to serve the church as well. As Matt Smethurst observes,

> Various religions in history have acknowledged the value of humility; none has dared speak of a humble God. The notion of humility applied to deity is simply seen as category confusion. So the claim that the God of the Bible—not a member of a pantheon, not an option on a menu of deities, but the one Creator of all—that he would stoop to serve his creatures, all the way down to a torturous cross, is not just startling; it's scandalous. . . . Lift your eyes from the mundane to the Messiah. See him touching unclean hands and washing filthy

feet and serving ungrateful sinners and finally relinquishing his life for those he loves. The entire shape of diaconal service finds its model and its mission in the life of your Savior.[10]

If you're a deacon already, then I hope you recognize the high and holy calling you've embraced. Your service reflects Christ's own service. Diaconal work is often exhausting, thankless work. I know keeping the church grounds, cleaning the kitchen, running the sound board, and making sure the food pantries are stocked doesn't feel like glamorous ministry. But in these acts of service, you're showing people something of the heart of your Savior. You're reflecting the care and devotion of the great Suffering Servant.

Diaconal work is anything but menial. It's a high and holy calling.

So What Now?

Let me conclude with a few encouragements for different types of folks who might be reading this book.

First, if you're not a deacon, let me encourage you to take note of the deacons in your church. Are they "full of the Spirit and of wisdom" (Acts 6:3)? Are they humbly and faithfully serving the church by providing for needs and preserving church unity? Then why not *tell them* what you see? Encourage them. Let them know how you appreciate what they do. Let them know that they model what a Christlike heart of service looks like.

But . . . don't stop there. Roll up your sleeves and get to work. Ask them if there's any way you can help. Ask if there's anything you should be doing to help shoulder the load.

Some of you reading this should aspire to become a deacon. Start by cultivating the character Paul commands in 1 Timothy 3 and by proving to be a model servant in your local church. Perhaps add each qualification to your regular quiet time.

Second, I want to talk to those who are already serving as deacons but have realized you're not exactly living up to the biblical model. Perhaps you've never understood your role this way. If that describes you, then now's the time to course correct. Reassess your responsibilities at church in light of what we studied above and consider how your life can more closely conform to Scripture. Ask your pastor or your elders for help on this. Invite them to shepherd you through these changes.

Third, you may have come to the end of this booklet and realized that, though you're a deacon, you actually desire to be an elder. You not only love studying God's word, you love teaching it, and you enjoy helping others apply it to their lives.

Paul reminded Timothy that "if anyone aspires to the office of overseer, he desires a *noble task*" (1 Tim. 3:1). Humbly let your pastors know you desire to be a shepherd, and then go on quietly doing the work of a deacon. Love the congregation, serve the church, disciple others, evangelize unbelievers, and, sure, teach as the Lord gives you the opportunity. Again, as you do, follow the counsel of your pastor or your elders. Invite them to shepherd you as you think through this aspiration.

Fourth, if you're already a deacon and you've been serving in the ways I described, then let me simply say "thank you." I want you to understand how valuable you are to your church. Remember, the ascended Christ has structured his church to suit it for its mission. Deacons are his idea. You have the vital role of protecting and prioritizing the church's mission as you preserve and promote the church's unity.

So brothers and sisters, thank you for your faithful ministry! To you is given a promise: deacons who have served well acquire for themselves a good standing and a great confidence in the faith that is in Christ Jesus (1 Tim. 3:13).

Recommended Resources

Thabiti Anyabwile, *Finding Faithful Elders and Deacons* (Wheaton, IL: Crossway, 2012).

Benjamin L. Merkle, *40 Questions about Elders and Deacons.* (Grand Rapids, MI: Kregel, 2008).

Matt Smethurst, *Deacons: How They Serve and Strengthen the Church* (Wheaton, IL: Crossway, 2021).

Alexander Strauch, *Paul's Vision for Deacons: Assisting the Elders with the Care of God's Church* (Littleton, CO: Lewis & Roth Publishers, 2017).

Notes

1. Personal stories involving other individuals are shared in this booklet with permission. Often pseudonyms have been used for privacy.
2. For more on how deacons function as assistants to the elders see Alexander Strauch, *Paul's Vision for the Deacons: Assisting the Elders with the Care of God's Church* (Littleton, CO: Lewis and Roth Publishers, 2017).
3. For a helpful explanation of the role of elders in the local church, see Jeramie Rinne, *Church Elders: How to Shepherd God's People Like Jesus* (Wheaton, IL: Crossway, 2014).
4. The terms *elders*, *pastors*, and *overseers* are used interchangeably in the New Testament to refer to the same office (Acts 20:17, 28; 1 Tim. 3:1; Titus 1:5, 7).
5. For a more thorough treatment of the qualifications of deacons, see Matt Smethurst, *Deacons: How They Serve and Strengthen the Church* (Wheaton, IL: Crossway, 2021), 53–65.

6. Matt Smethurst has done a fair job of laying out the arguments for both sides in his excellent book on deacons. See Smethurst, *Deacons*, 129–46.

7. See Alex Duke, "On Apple Stores and the DMV: Two Kinds of Churches that Create Complementarian Chaos" 9Marks, December 11, 2019, https://www.9marks.org/article/on-apples-stores-and-the-dmv-two-kinds-of-churches-that-create-complementarian-chaos/.

8. It is not the focus of this book to address the office of elders, much less make the case for only faithful men as pastors. For the argument that the office of pastor is limited to faithful men, see Andreas J. Köstenberger and Thomas R. Schreiner, eds., *Women in the Church: An Interpretation and Application of 1 Timothy 2:9–15*, 3rd ed. (Wheaton, IL: Crossway, 2016).

9. Smethurst, *Deacons*, 121.

10. Smethurst, *Deacons*, 127.

Scripture Index

IX 9Marks

Building Healthy Churches

9Marks exists to equip church leaders with a biblical vision and practical resources for displaying God's glory to the nations through healthy churches.

To that end, we want to see churches characterized by these nine marks of health:

1. Expositional Preaching
2. Gospel Doctrine
3. A Biblical Understanding of Conversion and Evangelism
4. Biblical Church Membership
5. Biblical Church Discipline
6. A Biblical Concern for Discipleship and Growth
7. Biblical Church Leadership
8. A Biblical Understanding of the Practice of Prayer
9. A Biblical Understanding and Practice of Missions

Find all our Crossway titles and other resources at 9Marks.org.

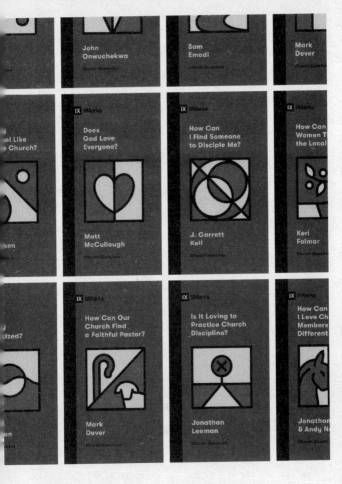

John
Onwuchekwa

Church Questions

Sam
Emadi

Church Questions

Mark
Dever

Church Questions

el Like
Church?

sen

Does
God Love
Everyone?

Matt
McCullough

Church Questions

How Can
I Find Someone
to Disciple Me?

J. Garrett
Kell

Church Questions

How Can
Women T
the Local

Keri
Folmar

Church Questions

ized?

on

How Can Our
Church Find
a Faithful Pastor?

Mark
Dever

Church Questions

Is It Loving to
Practice Church
Discipline?

Jonathan
Leeman

Church Questions

How Can
I Love Ch
Members
Different

Jonathan
& Andy N

Church Questions

IX 9Marks Church Questions

Providing ordinary Christians with sound and
accessible biblical teaching by answering
common questions about church life.

For more information, visit crossway.org.